MADE VISIBLE

by

Natalie Safir

Singular Speech Press

ACKNOWLEDGMENTS

Across the Sands *Slant* 1988 (published as: Poem Just Before the End)

Approaching the Solstice *Small Pond Magazine* 1988

Ancestry *Roh Wedder: An International Journal of Literature and Art* 1991-1992

Tribute to Henry Moore *Roh Wedder* 1992

Private Lives *Hudson Valley Echoes* 1992

Morning Service by the River *Pivot* 1992

Matisse's Dance I *The McGraw-Hill Book of Poetry*, by R. DiYanni and K. Rompf, 1993, McGraw-Hill Book Company, College Division; *Literature*, McGraw-Hill College Division, 1994; *Responding to Literature* (Third Edition), J. Stanford, Mayfield Pub., 1998

Ice Floats *Hudson Valley Echoes* 1993

Remedies *Poets On* 1993

Onus *Slant* 1994

House for Sale *The MacGuffin* 1994

The Still Point *Slant* 1994

Cover photograph: "Mast" 1991,
Courtesy of the photographer, Jonathan Safir

ISBN 1-880286-40-8

Singular Speech Press
Don D. Wilson, Editor/Publisher
Ten Hilltop Drive
Canton, Connecticut 06019

To the memory of my brother, Robert Safir
(May 29, 1926 to September 25, 1995)

THE FINAL ALLIANCE

Elegy for my brother

During his last weeks,
I tried to release him from
the death-field of the father; turn
him toward our mother's good power.

But allegiance to title and Book
held him in a deadly grip
as mother-blood (structural, lasting)
had strengthened him.

In the end the father seemed to claim him.

Now at graveside, late September
leaves stirring allow me
to know that out there,
returned to the electric stars,

mother and son embrace.

CONTENTS

I.   AS REFLECTIONS

II.   THE OTHER EYE

III.   RESEMBLANCES

... who could have thought to make
So many selves, so many sensuous worlds,
As if the air, the mid-day air, was swarming
With the metaphysical changes that occur,
Merely in living as and where we live.

— Wallace Stevens
from "Esthetic du Mal"

... to lie down by a slow river
and stare at the light in the trees —
to learn something by being nothing
a little while but the rich
lens of attention.

— Mary Oliver
from "Entering the Kingdom"

THIS YEAR WOMAN TREE

She never had flounces and frills like that —
            internal ruffles of orange, gold
light glistening in all her glad rooms.
            She never filled the window
with such positive posture,
            the distance between her widening shape
and the copper beech closing
            on its way to the river.

The first to flower orange and the first
            to fall, I used to say, fearing
for her short life of passion.
            Now light holds her and she
holds the light, while the trunk
            inside, branching like a transit line
sends up every shade the minerals of life
            provide — lemons, apple greens,
earth charcoals and winter browns.

THE WOMAN AND THE TREE

Yellow jewels are falling
from her arms and shoulders.
The woman sees the tree shimmy
in delight to shake them free.
Air ruffles her sleeves.

***

Absence of wind.
The base of the tree holds
everything she has given up.
As if her attention lights them,
the leaves bask in her favor.

***

No yellows, only exposed browns
tone foreground. The tree
is an upended pitchfork
railing and ashamed of her nakedness.
Her outrage shouts:
what has it all been for?

***

Bleak stillness.
No longer willing to review
her high days of color,
she freezes, brittle and gray
beside the black fence.

***

Late November. The woman
passing hardly recognizes her—
an iron candelabra
alone in the dark.

SISTERS

White sister, dark —
who carries emptiness to the bowl?
Who drains the drink
then cracks the cup?
Who leads the dog
to a barren lair, whines
with the dog when
the larder is bare?

Dark sister, white —
who fans the stars
then drenches their fires?
Who crowns the dress, smashes the jewel,
finds space for the missing rings?
Who houses the swan,
banishes wolves, then beckons them
back to the hearth.
Who sets the trap but
loosens the springs
of the rabbit snare?

White sister, dark
riding an arc between forest
and shore — who offers less,
promises more?

TO THE FIELD

I went to a field
in the late afternoon
to find quiet

To see what stands

I went to a field
to lose the pressure of purpose,
enter time without hours

To see the bent, the broken, and all
that on the brink of winter, waits

Trees that grow just by standing,
sky that moves but goes nowhere

Here as the low rays slant
across the field, a rise
of golden orange takes me out
of my losses into a vast wondering

Quiet comes to my body

It is the trees that tell me —
Stand for a while, feel, see

Forgive yourself

DARK SQUIRREL

Color of rain-soaked treebark, tail
edged by lightning sparks, he
hopped through bare branches
munching shell scraps, and

for a split second on
the branch, fixed a curious look
on me, so I had the chance
to see —
throbbing like a live berry —
the fiery little heart
that propelled him.

The sight of it
trembling with urgency, exposed
so close to the surface — I had to
look away.

WOMAN BEFORE A FULL LENGTH MIRROR

First the careful evaluation
of breast shape, blush and tilt of nipples,
sideways and with arms raised,
then down the scope of waist, mound
of belly, plump curve
leading outward to hips.
She examines the flats of her back,
angle and swell of buttocks, dimples
and depressions in her flesh.
Shaded spots, veins bluing
the skin, each indelible
blemish demanding her scrutiny.

Her eyes sneak into the hollow of her arms
where dark hairs lie hidden, then
quickly dart to her head and
return to peruse curls
faintly shadowing the winged vee
between her thighs. She arranges
her legs this way, that, each angle
offering another revelation.

At her knees she stops, familiar
enough with the line to ankle.

What did he mean, exactly, that
a woman's unclothed body matches
her face's history, when each
records wear so differently?

Stripped, she lingers,
flushed as the mirror wavers.

ANESTHESIA

I have been taken from you
by the cool needle
and we have been parted
for the first time
since we were born.

You rolled away
on a pale stretcher
and I, lost into a white hole
had to trust you'd go on
without me.

Surgeons removed what you
needed to lose and I lost
a piece two and a half
hours wide, cut out
for all time.

When my eyes, light pins,
reattach and I repeat
my name, rings taped
to my fingers,

we are
returned.

THE STILL POINT

I'm standing in the 98 degree heat
of father's day with this grown son, listening:
"Like some kind of brain stutter,
my old grade-school chum picked up
the conversation we were having
in third grade, each of us standing
in the gym with our little sons.
Some kind of brain pause, him talking
like it was still today,"
John reports, and I'm thinking:
part of it still is today,
the still point in motion bio-physicists
describe, that self taking itself all
the way to the present.

I see motorboats on the Hudson
zipping along, sailboats skimming slowly;
they will all arrive at the same point.

Brain and blood's boiling in that heat,
bubbling it all back up till my head
nears explosion. Miles away,
my daughter Allison's about to bury
her fiance's mother whose brain
exploded unexpectedly in Florida
by the sea. Time's up.

They grieve and grieve while
her organs board a jetplane
to rescue someone else in ICU.
They don't yet understand the story
that wants to keep going on and on.

"Get me a cool glass of water,"
Aunt Mary said to my mother
as a child. Returning, she found
her aunt gone, a smile lighting her face.
Time's up. Time's out.

What a beautiful death, my mother
in her eighties remembers, what a beautiful death.

WINDS
        — for my daughter Eliza

When rain comes through
a trap-door opening,
flogging windows, cars, the lawn —
trees luxuriating in fullness of the bath —
and skysound strikes heavy blows,
I revel in the scale of the drama,
knowing that life's excesses,
unexpected floods and fires
come like that.

Last night my youngest drove off in a truck
to settle in the Midwest.
It should have been a night of winds,
but the July stillness offered
the nothingness of holes,
parts of myself going off
into humid air trailed by goodbyes and gifts.

I am not ready for this rite of passage,
for my daughter to make her home
a man I hardly know, his people,
a city only imagined in its rhythmic
click of syllables.

Cincinnatus, I've read, was the only Roman emperor
who returned power to his people —
a leader of simple virtue this city
on the Ohio took for its name.

My daughter's skin is fair, freckles
like summer peaches and burns easily.
I want her protected.

In the hall closet, I search around for
the large blue umbrella.

10

HOUSE FOR SALE

The foaming, billowing sky
that wrapped around the house
told her winter's story
waited in the air.
She left the car, paced
to the thinning evergreens
in the back, noticed
how small the house had become.
Siding flaps had worn,
gutters were bent with rust.

No one had removed the dead woman's
things, prayer cards still
on the bedside table, coverlet
rumpled, pillow dented.
No one had covered the mirrors,
removed doilies from armchairs.
An anniversary card tacked up
in the kitchen told of the last family party.
No one had turned the lights back on.

The sky covering the house
like a white tide
told her winter waited for her
and all the winters
that would arrive on blades,
with purifying stings and scrapes.
She would choose this place
for days of diamond brightness, for
slow nights trailing off
into frosted smoke.

STRONGER THAN BLACK PAINT

The night our bodies
brought surprise glories,

over my flesh, a spread of light
showered colors stronger
than black paint shadowing our map.

Sweet were the uses of what we made,
urging me to travel:

Travel again
with your head uncovered.

SYZYGY

My pubic hairs grow
back dark and spiky
below cross-stitches
where my flesh was cut.

I'm on my back staring
at cracked plaster.
Your body at cross-purposes
above, aimed at entry.
Nothing opens, the ceiling
doesn't lift.

What became of the two luminous
planets co-ordinating
earlier this month
about twinkly skies?

Black ice moments
drizzle on us.

At the window,
shiny little daggers.

THE CAVE

Quickly they enter the cave.

In the brown light their bodies are branches,
angles and arcs that stretch for connection;

in the brown cave their bodies
are ropes knotted and twisting;

in the sweet cave their bodies
are soil sifting together;

in the deep cave their bodies
are boulders that interlock.

Then she is all cave
and he is all waterfall.

She is cave, deep mouth of the dark
and height of the waterfall,

and no one else lives in the world.

OUR RED KITE

The kite could not rise
though you ran with it
from the tallest dune.

A sleek red spear, it plunged
nose first again and again,
tail shivering,

until we ran it together, my hands
gripping the cordspool, yours
hoisted high toward the sun.

Then, up over the clear green sea,
we let it out, we let it
out and it climbed jerkily,
reaching heights — a smaller
and smaller daredevil rising.

                    ***
We didn't see it dive,
just bits of red peeking in
and out of seafoam. We
pulled hard to tug back
our doomed runaway.

You kept winding, carefully
counting till the cordspool fattened
and a drenched, battered
form flopped to the sand.

I wanted to stroke it,
chant a restorative prayer, but

snappily, you dusted it off,
neatly packed the string-bobbin

into the trunk of our car,
tucked in the sky diver

until the next run.

SEPARATING

Rodents can die
if they cannot chew on something
and some men die if they are closed
in cages; women, if they do not have
a love that feeds the milk flow.

What is expected and desired
has to be sectioned off
from what is given.

So I am separating
the circle on the table
where the drink sits from
the white ring inside the glass.

I'm dead center in a dry field
as one feather floats to my hands.

A grey mouse scurries about, nosing
into dirt clumps. A cat tenses.

Rodents slide out of their corners
to find what to chew.

TWO KINDS OF DANGER

Rotted peaches lie about
like bombs about to detonate.
Two marsh-hawks hang midair
numbed by the haze.

These Indian summer days, some
creature swoops talons first
toward my still mind —
easy prey for an assault.

Diving, it strafes a tree,
frightens my mind to rush
into thickets, where hiding,
it encounters the predator within —
the one that can turn itself
into the hunter and the hunted.

BARRIERS

Cat on the sill, still as she
watches night work its tricks.

A woman's eye connecting one tree trunk
to another creates a plane where spirits dance.

Between storm window and screen, air
is locked out, permanently sealed in.

If the young man inquires about the flow
of my life, I'll deny barriers, lying.

Dark blue diamonds in the oriental rug
graze angled sides, shift, enter one another.

ICEFLOATS - Hudson Highlands

The dawn bell floats toward me
at the riverbank
as a light-field of forgiveness.

Clouds open, lift. Fingers to my lips,
I hear the tumble of riverwater, slow
creak and groan of icefloats plodding upstream.

And between, in a ripple of silvers,
a slim rush travels back.

So much solace in the sight of this river
flowing both ways —
dull drumbeats that mark the slow advance north —
the blunt thrum no matter what,

and the fevered burble that hurries back.

Ice memories. The flow and
the return.

ACROSS THE SANDS

At some point you can even stop kicking the horse,
his carcass prone, vital signs lost,
odor of life still rife about the flesh.

You were trying to rouse him.

Heavy corpse on your bedroom floor,
great head quiet, sluggish eyes
no longer rolling. Sense
in your hands warns — let him go;
blood in your fingers
reaches out to revive him.

You remember handing him sugar bits,
how his soft lip curled over and around,
muzzle smooth as mouseskin,
supple as dough.
Days you offered him alfalfa sprouts,
the snowy crunch of a new apple,
his jaws rocking side to side
the way a porchswing moves.
                              But the horse

is dead, supine on your carpet,
a melt of chestnut hide glistening
to remind you of canters at dawn,
the two of you on a wild plum beach flying
across moist sand. Breadth
of his shoulder muscles
rolling under the flesh as if
they would always endure. The horse

is dead. Sugar, not kicking kept him going.

You dream him standing tall at the gate,
hocks quivering, ready to run.
You dream his throaty neigh, your legs
pressed against his flanks.

Dead flesh reeks on your carpet.

How long ago did you
ride the sands together?

My galloping memory —

REGRET IS NOT A RIVER

Everyone, he said to me,
needs branches and mirrors.
Yet the tentacles that grab
from the deep, the reviewed self
that flashed from eyes and
lips of others, can become
dangerously thick
as the underwebbing of lilypads.

I remember circling
in a flat-bottom boat with him,
how we became caught
in the lily-weavings and began
to paddle backwards.
Always, I thought, we will always
be trapped in what he cannot give,
what I cannot accept.

An eyeball trained on the flotsam
of words and gestures sees all
we might have set afloat into the sun.

What is missed is missed and
regret is not a river,
but a dark-skinned lake.

I lean from the boat, foolishly
bend toward a reflection
thin as the shimmer of youth.

LIGHT AND DEATH

I've had the report about tumors
lodged in the neck of my old cat —
longtime companion,
gentlest of the old mothers.

On this longest day of light,
her body stretches like a scarf
across a wide threshold.
She watches only the door.

I cling to the late light,
the pale green of her eyes, and
imagine holding her as the doctor
eases her into sleep.

Little by little, light slips away.
Green deepens to forest dark. I know
I'll be able to carry her
across, almost weightless in my arms.

PRIVATE LIVES
— for Phyllis

October disappears earlier each day.
Clusters of days repeating
in the swirl and spread of leaves.

In the chill smokiness, I still hear you
calling in your dogs
from frisking through leaf piles,

the clang of your iron kettle
against burner grates, crinkle
of wrappers from the biscuit tin.

We talked urgently over so many pots of tea.
Whose need clamored more fiercely for attention?

Two women, whose private lives leapt
from our skins out into the mulberry dusk.

In the chill smokiness I hear
the timbre of your call.

Fire beetles blink on and off in the foliage,
flecks and tints of their lives soon lost.

Through leaf-rustle and crunch, you walk
toward me, your eyes gold cinders.

AUTUMN EQUINOX

As I sit down in the morning
to mourn my dead brother,
the currency of achievement,
labor and energy, enters my thoughts
before the shaded corridor
I must approach to meet him.

One cat hunched on the sofa under the lamp
faces the wall, the other toward the room.
With the departing season, expect the next.
Turn one way to embrace the dark; rearrange
yourself and light can push through.

At my table, a young woman writes "eyes to toes."
Another, older, sees death's beauty
in crumpled Panamanian lilies.
A hummingbird whirs above a threshold.

Like muscular trees extending from one broad trunk,
sisters of morning and dusk lock arms.

I have thrown open many doors, removed
skins from windows, and wait to walk through.

From the old Bible, I read: Comfort me with apples.
Greenings, goldens will do.
The plump sorrow of the winesap.

ANCESTRY

If it wasn't Emma Bovary's white thighs I slid from,
then Tolstoi's Anna opened her legs to push me out.
In the darkened room where flames choked, where bearded,
cloaked men stood mumbling, the stately clock
declared its dominance — the rustle of silks
a dream shredded on the spokes of time.

Out onto the tracks, into the path of the locomotive
roaring, clamor of train iron, momentum of metal.

Sparks flew onto the frozen snow to signal the birth.
Onto bleached white sheets, fresh blood splattering.

MATISSE'S "DANCE I"

A break in the circle dance of naked women,
dropped stitch between the hands
of the slender figure stretching too hard
to reach her joyful sisters.

Spirals of glee sail from the arms
of the tallest woman. She pulls
the circle around with her fire.
What has she found that she doesn't
keep losing, her torso
a green-burning torch?

Grass mounds curve ripely beneath
two others who dance beyond the blue.
Breast swell and multiply and
rhythms rise to a gallop.

Hurry, frightened one and grab on — before
the stitch is forever lost, before the dance
unravels and a black sun swirls from that space.

MATISSE'S "DANCE II"

We would stop if we could stop turning
before the boiled sun drops.
Our muscles are twists of tangled rope.
The more we pull the tighter the tangle.

We women have lost our sex.
I lower my head to a belly distended,
to sparse hairs of my pudendum,
a cleft of dryness below.

We are used beyond repair,
tired beyond ambition. We grow
shabby with trying while
the plundering beat ravages us.

Will it never be done?
Is there no release from the ring?

CEZANNE'S "HOUSE WITH THE CRACKED WALLS"

I.

The house with cracked walls
stands.
The squamous sky and torn trees
cannot unsettle the foundation.

Where the earth parts and
the steep shelf rises,
I hear a whisper underground:

Let me stand the way
the cracked house stands —
facing the vagaries of weather —
not lying to myself
or anyone else.

II.

The cracked house stands
despite its cracks.
(Every time she looked
at the painting she knew.)

Trees ragged
in a churning blue sky
stoop on spindly legs.

(She sees the earth cleave
and throw up a boulder; that
the eyes of the house stare in terror.)

TRIBUTE TO HENRY MOORE

Through vaulted haunch,
pelvic cradle
scooped and socketed,
basso tones echo
caves of the ancients,
oxen bone in the jaw of the dog.

Woman reclines
on the slim boundary of origin.
Turning, she is prone
to rise
from a base of rock.

Without spear or prop
she wears only
her flesh as armor —

The grace and girth of her frame
a testament to her position.

Rising, she towers —
A cascade of amplitude.

RED

BOATS OF SAINT MARIE
      — from a painting by Vincent VanGogh

The moored trawlers are awkward, pinched
boots left behind on a pebbly shore.
Twiglike masts stretch toward
sister ships out in the channel's widewaters.
Their folded sails implore the wind
to dispatch them to distant
red splotches on bluegem seas.

But they remain beached.
Taut lines angle to the wind's howl.
Weathered wood creaks from its carcass,
straining toward the vast opening.

THE RED DOOR
      (from a painting by Georgia O'Keeffe)

She wanted to pass through the blood zone,
fiery square on the face of an old building
without handle or hinge.
Her eye pushed through it before her will.

Months later in the red storm of her dying,
she heaved against it,
glimpsed the other side, with
bold strokes from the scorch of sunset.

31

ROTHKO: TWO NUDES

A sweaty compression connects them.
The glue of unavoidable involvement.

An orange woman with clublike feet,
chair legs looks left.
Behind her — hairy, coarse
and bear brown, the second woman
stares too, her breath at the nape
of the other's neck. Heavy, heavier.

(My colored soul, her shaggy hair,
my ripening flesh, her gnarled teeth,
my windy eyes, her gnashing jaw.)

VUILLARD'S INTERIORS

Bird-bone hands of his sister
push needles through fabric;
moving closer, his mother's spidery breath
binds thread about his ankles.

Tapestry walls of the sitting room
paper his sunless days.
He would never try to leave.

He's a crippled mole in love
with his garden, dragging
little brush marks up
and back through the soil.

Surely Madame will have an outing
today if her pointed black shoes
and fur piece are brought to her.

Maman! cries the sister, tell Edouard
he must join us here
enjoying our fine cakes.

Tell Edouard he must join us.

RICHARD BOSMAN'S "WINTER RIVER"

Woodcut: four winter scenes arranged as one

Is each the same winter river? —
carving out its shape,
inclined to the headlands where moonlight
glosses the climb, then in descent,
rapid as a spill of dice.

Do the four scenes connect as narrative?
My life a steel blue haze
at the start, then clarifying
so I see myself
against a backdrop of four directions,
water, sky and land wedged
to form a decade.

Looking back: my river turns
brazen in the sun's long rays,
then bleak in a rain of hailstones.
Black teeth of the hemlock
narrow the shores.
Channels deepen and
the long land behind grows dimmer.

The Hudson Highlands
in biting relief — four icy rivers turning,
jagged stands of hemlock,
hills shaggy as bearded buffalo,
a sky of snowdrifts.

VISIT TO THE "MODERN" - Three paintings

Something must be said
of the glaze shining apple skins
in the Cezanne painting. Radiant praise.
Mastery of pigment. But rhetoric
cannot approach that vibrant patch.
Squeeze out a tube of cadmium red.
Say "red, red, red." Speech or
its lack does not restrain that red.

***

Sitting before Monet's waterlilies,
I stare at consolation falsely prolonged.
Nor could such silence last. Monet's faith
floats those pads onto sympathetic waters.
An old man enveloped in misty morning,
the hush before evening. My task
is to survive the sun's entire tour.

***

In Rousseau's jungle panorama
the eye of night opens wide. A lion
licks the man awake to the nightmare and
already other beasts are active.

I would trade my perception gladly
for the sizzle of sun on apples, or
a benign haze above the lilypond, trade
it gladly for a child's eye, aware
of only one corner of the sprawling canvas.

POSTURES

Here is the mouth speaking,
here is the body moving sideways,
a limp soldier defecting
while will trembles and
becomes a cone of hay;
then mind shifts into dance,
spirit mounts a horse and
flies over a tornado.

Split! the self demands
in position at the ballet bar.
All exercises and arabesques
have been executed with discipline.
Remorse has turned to well-toned muscle.

Here is the torso turning
while the spine stands at attention.
Here is the mirror watching
the two of them embrace
shouting "liar"
with her three lips.

IF MULES ARE SLIPPERS

— for women only

If Anus were bumpy legumes grown in Honduras,
Hemorrhoids might be New Age musical instruments,
Then Uterus lies next to the solenoid under my carhood,
And Vulva is a mutant hepatica thriving in the Plain States.

Vagina ruled Merrie Olde England in the 1300's,
Pubis the purple stone of royalty loved by the populace.
Clitoris is a form of enameling perfected by the Persians,
Cervix the FDA seal on over-the-counter pain killers.

Fibroids are bi-valves sought after by the Portuguese,
The Fallopian Tubes connect downtown Rome to the Appian Way.
Placenta are heavy workboots with velcro closures.

A recently discovered work by Handel is titled
"The Ovarian Suite," and the House of
Lancôme's latest fragrance hails as "Amniocentesis."

Femininity is flame retardant tinsel recommended for yule trees
and Maternities are investment instruments
touted by Yuppies, Wannabees, and Gottagets.

ARMS FULL OF IRIS

With the surprise and apology
of one finding herself alone
at a grand party, but into whose life
a profuse gift of affection
has suddenly been thrust, the plain
woman in late middle age
holds an armful of long-stemmed iris
just about to come apart.

Surrounding her face — pale peach
frills and ruffled edges,
perfume of old English drawing rooms.

Holding them, she looks at me
as if to ask a question.

Don't I have my own fragilities
to carry and cherish?

EACH TIME
        — for Leo

No two sunset skies streaking are alike,
        nor slate formations just before
the downpour, and each end-of-summer rose
        has a slight alteration to its face.

And the beloved's face is like no other,
        nor the way we entered the sea
each morning — with sudden shout and plunge
        or slowly without sound or splash.

We sat beside Shinnecock Canal watching
        pleasure boats stream through —
each beaming crew and cargo, a show
        of flags flapping, freshly painted names.

As we returned many afternoons to follow
        the turning ribbon of boats,
we too shifted on the banks, the sun splitting
        into lengthening strands of color.

No two sunset skies streaking are alike,
        nor slate formations just before
the downpour, and each rose at summer's end
        must face unending alterations.

ONE WOULD LIKE TO FIND

It had to be a short, cold summer,
with snow in June. They tried
slowly turning back the clock,
from tough life
to a disappearing era — safe
from assault, busy with renewal,
innocent that values and people collide,
that skin color turns unavoidable,
that governments become
a muddy series of "who dunnits"
and trust unravels across the land.

Small solace, then, to find some sacred place
where a river runs. Little consolation
on a summer night gone wrong to get
carried away by glorious feathers.
One would like to be newly in love
entering a green phrase; one would like
to find, as snowflakes come down,
sparklers in grass and equal love
indivisible for once and for all.

Snow in June is a plague of winter wasps.

INVISIBLE PILOT

Small in the midst of the great alone,
the invisible pilot of a white sailboat
skims over the water's weavings
in a strip of private bliss.

Who, out there?
And who is the solitary gull
riding that morning river of rapture?

The extra hour that drops into our hands
tonight offers a timeless chance
to repeat, alter, or hold ...

a trembling kitten, Ravel's urgent ecstasies,
the old moments when love was just
starting — desire

flashing from a man's eyes —
whitecaps that warned of dangerous crossings.

NOVEMBER DIRECTIVE

Whatever eccentricities of light
announce themselves:

sharp fricatives on rainy pavement,
heels scraped over a sewer grating,
brakes and horns in fierce combat,
an old woman's fiery cackle,

watery brights in a child's eyes —

must hold foreground against the bleak.

REMARKS

Witch-claw moon
incisor sharp, whisker bright,
strikes remarks into winter sky

First: that love is long
and pins the will into submission

Second: the slit of the feline eye
slides straight to the vein of the heart

Hold my wrist — it is leaking

A WAY HOME

It's foolish to worry about the great snows
of winters gone — they float across
parkways, slip into storm drains,
slide down hillsides like graceful ghosts.

This morning the white hills lost
their dye to the roads, exposed
brown tufts raw as a newborn.

Snow piles weep back into the earth's lap
and I wonder, warm in your embrace, if
my tears will find a way home.

EQUINOX

in memory of my mother, Bessie Dorfman Safir

The day dark is long
as light or daylight
is long as dark is
the time to stand
equally on two feet and
regard the continuous line
that changes from this form
first into that form last
changing with the same
but altered face so
all pictures line up side
by side the length of
the wall and the baby touches
the tomboy girl the serious bride
beside a fleshy woman the old woman
all found and lost in her and
the changing does not stop
even at that perfect meeting-
ground of day and dark
even after some specific body
makes no move under
the lid of the box
lowered
in daylight
into dark

ONUS

Men spit on streets; once
I saw a man blow his nose out
a car window. A crow big as an alleycat
was picking at the red strings
of a crushed squirrel in the road.
Pulling and stretching string by string,
the body reduced to a pile of smeared pasta.

On the bay beach we walked, I couldn't
bear crunching periwinkle shells
that pebbled the salt flats
though their profusion allowed me
to care less. And if you stamped hard
long gray squirts from dime-sized holes
shot up to splatter you.

Life is this slimy. Seamus Heaney confessed
his boyhood revulsion at thick frog spawn;
Edmund Wilson, in his 70s wrote about combing
brown slime from his tongue. The bug-eyed bull terrier
that frolicked to meet me today slobbered all over my leg.

I consider wetness. Pungent, lubricating goos
of sex, the mouth's insides slippery as seafood.
"Fruits de Mer" slurped from the lips,
ripe plum nectars, gauzy peach,
erotica of the mango, pearly membranes,
our noses filling with emissions.

Fishermen plunge their fingers behind
gills to pull away sinews of the heart.
The heavy afterbirth my daughter expelled
was thick with bloodgel as rank beefsteak.

Aesthetes and ladies in pale kimonos, tell me
where to go with this. Ribald heroes, urge me on.
How to find the teeming gelatinous ooze of life
more palatable than slops,
effluents discharged from our bodies
less onerous than death.

REMEDIES

The silver pan of morning catches nailheads
of rain, tap by tap and I see you
beached on your sickbed,
restless with wings of flying horses.

Care — the word — water in a clear jar,
surprises me, and the appearance of white tulips,
stems the height of cranes,
heads lowered in silence.

Now the lustrous woman in Vermeer's painting
stands beside you, pitcher glinting
on the table, a widening of honeyed light
so delicate, motes sparkle in it.
            The scene domestic —
as if in banishing the solitary
from this writing, I bring
lemons to your lips,
and a feather.

DECEMBER SNOWSTORM

I seem to love snow without reason.
Born in the middle of winter, I burrow
now like the resting bear — a land woman —
far from the river closing over.

A smooth isolation of high drifts
erases paths, drapes windows.

Rather than stroke fur, lift the phone,
kiss a shoulder, I find solace
within a solitary mountain —
something locked inside this crystal silence
that does not push against any door
or seek to tunnel out to others.

Should I feel victorious, or fearful?
Rest with this quiet, or

rush outside, lift my face to the cold?

MORNING SERVICE BY THE RIVER

Sun hits the belly of the gull
before it warms our shoulders.

We stand in a circle by the old river,
cold in our shoes, arms touching.

Sun heat lifts the wild geese.
Gulls cross and recross, sail air
as light tints villages on the hill.

One by one, we each pitch a stone
into the forgiving river that
swallows and sinks our burdens.

With different notes of the same word,
the old river answers.
Gulls voice their flight.

Over our singular and common faces,
sky spreads the great gift of blue.

TREE LIFE

Days after the hurricane
      ripped tops off hundreds of trees
on the Cape — limbs strewn about
      lawns and fields — a giant carcass
torn from broken ground,
      orange earth still clinging
to tangled root wires,
      lay on its side.

This was the core of the creature:
      unruly underside, a fester of coils
whose energy sent up the tall trunk,
      arms to bend and reach.

Forceful underground
      of consciousness
whose alchemy sends forth gestures,
      works of art.

AFTERNOONS OF THE WORLD

Late shadows stretch the lawn's length
A glaze of leaves in full dazzle

Abundance glittering

A young father sits on the lawn
with a toddler son, throwing and holding
a red ball the little boy chases

People indoors prepare the evening meal,
complete details, recount news

The sun slides over the edge as it must

So much has come before me
So much will come after me

Is a gleam of leaves against
shaggy spruce — seen and
relished, enough?

What else do I need — to believe I can
summon this scene
when despair takes over?

I hold to the mosaic before me —
rocket black shoots of shadow burst
in and out of lemon light —

For the moment, it almost
displaces hunger's terrible teeth

APPROACHING THE SOLSTICE

Great crows slowly wheel
through a streaked sky

Long swathes of snow
across a blue backdrop

Who collects the tire-crushed animals
jelly-gutted on local roads
before we start for work?

That's Matisse's blue, filled
with a hidden sun

Weathermen are promising a mild Christmas
following daylight's shortest span,
no blanket of purity to cover
whatever sorrows shade the roads

The lament for love lost frees
the soul to seek again

Song of what has been lost, what
will be lost, returns

Long arc of the glossy crow,
cool conviction of his flight
across my blue optimism

White, mixture of all possible light

His dark swoop, his piercing wing

GROWTH

Brown leaves crisp as cornflakes
fully shape this bush,
dry rattling in early April winds.

Brooks, seeping through soaked earth,
hurry toward the Hudson.
Buds show up on skeletal shoots.
Fields are swollen with greening.

And the bush, just as before,
carries its empty lanterns,
torn, illegible letters.

Still afraid to discard
what's already dead?

Old fool!

FOR WANT OF SNOW

1.

No one can say where a flake forms;
no one can see the moist bead that high
pick up goose and swansdown,
drop through passages of chill,
gathering wings, silence, singularity.

2.

Foliage down,
the spare branch allows insight
to lines of structure, so we
might see what lies beneath.

Little wonder the sparkle
of first flakes thrills us
with its fresh coat
of illusion.

3.

The sun, like a shy husband
approaching the snowy bed
of his wintry bride
timidly peers over her white torso
wondering how high he must rise
to warm her.

4.

For want of snow,
she sought out
moonlight, for lack
of moonlight, searched
for stars, for want of
stars, hunted flame,
lacking flame, raked
for embers, lacking
embers, scratched
for sparks, for want of
sparks, she dug below —

She mined for coal
for want of snow.

SNOW

One skin, one long undulation of skin,
porous and powdery while

the earth animal lies beneath
breathing through and into
this membrane of light.

The crush of my shoes makes tinsel music.
My eyes fill with white waves;
a rush of respiration
expands my seemingly solid self.

Could any other part of the universe
be this new? This night we begin again!

I am a galaxy of fresh flakes
collecting with invisible speed.

Across it, my blue shadow.